Gloria's Daughter

Gloria's Daughter

Jacque R. Cox

iUniverse, Inc.
New York   Bloomington

Gloria's Daughter

iUniverse books may be ordered through booksellers or by contacting:

iUniverse
1663 Liberty Drive
Bloomington, IN 47403
www.iuniverse.com
1-800-Authors (1-800-288-4677)

ISBN: 978-1-4401-6292-3 (pbk)
ISBN: 978-1-4401-6291-6 (ebk)

Printed in the United States of America

iUniverse rev. date: 8/26/2009

This book is dedicated to my loving husband Kurtis,

and my beautiful daughter Danika.

I couldn't have done this without the support

of my family and friends.

A Boy

A boy

Full of life

Endless possibilities

No headache or strife

The rippling water progressively grows

A making of new innocence

From within energy flows

Wondering about that reflection

A mirage or is this me

Now he gets older and full of emotion

A man he is and shall ever be

A Pot of Love

Love is a form of personal reaction
Your head is the center of intellect
Your eyes see the man you want most
Your nose smells the flowers he sent
Your ears need kind words and sentiments
Your facial expression of knowing he cares
Your hands work through benevolence
Your heart is the center of emotion
Your breast so tender to his touch
Your stomach has butterflies
Your knees shaking of that question he may ask
Your leg was touched by his hand for the first time
Your feet curled up with his in a nice warm bed

Alone

Do you know what it is like to feel so a lone
Coming home to an empty place everyday
A saddened face shall come my way
Being so afraid of the unknown

On a dark night
Driving under a street lamp
Noticing my reflection in the window
Wondering who that person is on the other side

Sitting in the plane on that one way flight
Small narrow seats legs getting a cramp
Starting over once again,
A single tear strolls down, hiding my face in the pillow
He said he loved me but then he lied

At the beach flying a kite
Walking and thinking, kicking the water getting so damp
Viewing from the distance a tree, a weeping willow
Weeping is what my heart feels inside

Do you know what it is like to feel so a lone
Coming home to an empty place everyday
A saddened face shall come my way
Being so afraid of the unknown

Because of You

Because of you I see truth in your hazel eyes

Because of you I want there to be no goodbyes

Because of you I feel safe and secure

Because of you I can relearn to relax and mature

Because of you, you captured my heart

Because of you I have a new start

Because of you my heart sings,

My soul rings,

My stomach has butterflies

Because of you I hope our friendship never dies

Because of a new found home, beautiful acres for miles and miles

I remember what it feels like to smile

Because of you I no longer harden my heart and swallow my tears

Because of you I have no fears

Being You

Sometimes things happen for a reason

Honestly no one knows why

You may be scared in your heart and mind

And for that matter you may always stay shy

You should search your feelings and find security within yourself

You will have, find, and achieve

Knowing your soul and being will never leave

You need to be no one else but you

Relish those feeling

And let it guide you to stay true

Help guide your self

Through the hard times

Have fun

Drink coronas but don't forget the limes

Describing a Wish

Fountain

Wish, synchronized

Inspiration, Beautiful, Spray

Clear, Sparkle, Oval, Pure

Rippling, Refreshing, Splattering

Drops, Wet

Water

Diamond

I
Me
Us & we
Futures to see
Together we shall be
Willing souls of he & she
Love should be respected with amity
Creatures of the heart live in peace for eternity
A diamond is a sign of beauty and perfection like love
A couple, the two of you will live long and happy
Stand together holding hands proudly
Eyes attached, see all beauty
On bended knee
Us & we
Me
I

Directions to Love

To find true love
And know he is your soul mate
Follow your heart
And let it guide you

Expression
Expression from his smile
Expression of his face
Express yourself

Truth
Truth of his eyes
Truth of your soul
Trust yourself

Follow
Follow your head
Follow your heart
Follow what your instinct tells you

Love
Love life
Love him
Love yourself

Figure of My Life

You are the figure of my life

I just don't think of you as a brother-in-law

I think of you as the man in my life

You are the figure of my life

You are the only man that has ever loved me the way I needed

From you; that love and gratitude made me into the person I am today

You are the figure of my life

The father I never had

The father I always wanted

You are the figure of my life

I want you to walk me down the path of life

Stand tall &

Give me away to the next man that deserves me

You are the figure of my life

You are my mentor

You are my protector

You are my friend

You are the figure of my life

Forever and a Day

I want to be your best friend
Forever and a day
I would have loved you as a child
I would have asked you out to play
I love you as a man
The way you are today
The brown in your hair
The clothes you wear
The things you do and say
I will love you forever
When your hair has turned to gray
When we've left this world
When our lives have passed away
I will have loved you forever
Forever and a day

Fork in the Road

Fork in the road

One path can lead to everything you have ever wanted

The other path can lead to more hard times

But endless possibilities

The path you choose is the most important

For your happiness

For your sanity

And for your heart

Endure the feelings of peace

With perfection comes ambition

Ambition comes with passion

Passion comes with hope

You can't live without hope

You just have to live

Garage Sale

Someone else's junk is another's treasure
Family traditions enjoying each other's company
Walking house to house browsing and looking
With so much pleasure
Nieces and nephews, brothers and sisters
Buying toys and they already have so many
Warm sunshine, tennis shoes for walking
Smiles on faces, grateful for this beautiful weather
Each garage sale is full of the unknown
The excitement and friendships will live on
Forever and ever

Gazebo

Sensible moments pondering under the gazebo;
While considering those unspoken words under the gazebo.

Acknowledge excellence of heart,
Beneath that shy exterior under the gazebo.

Eyes can tell more than one story,
Deliberating what they have told you under the gazebo.

What thought, that thought;
Thoughts collide together making sense of passion under the gazebo.

The question was clouded but the answer is clear,
Knowing it's love sitting under the gazebo.

Hunter

Run

Quick feet

Endurance

Breathe in and out

Each sprint at a time

Don't look back only forward

Go fast keep up the pace

Focus only on you not others

Being first is not what is important

Icicle

Heavy snowfall in mid-December

Icicles forming from the roof top

Drop by drop each gets longer

Frost bound glacial object

Cold weather conditions

Freezing, melting

Icicle

Ice

Intrigue

Listen to the words, and feel the music

Elapse the pain that consoles you

Let it trigger your heart and feed your soul

Grasp the love that is intriguingly true

The harmony of notes that flows through your body,

Makes you feel out of control

Music sharpens emotions and suppresses the mind

Love magnifies your spirit and embraces it's warmth

Life and love is both full of heartache and happiness

Granted makes the world so kind

John Deere

Tractor

green with heavy duty treads

harvesting crops

in the afternoon sun

a powerful machine

Journey of happiness

Life is full of many hardships and decisions that you have to make

Transitions that change your life forever

Loneliness and detriment flows within your heart

Being scared is a natural feeling, having courage means everything

Stand tall and proud

With your head held high

Smile

Warm your heart

Think no bitter thoughts

Life is full of many beautiful things

Love, honesty, trust, laughing

Followed with a warm heart

Only you can find what makes you happy

Have faith in yourself

Choose the right path and follow your destiny

Then shall you find peace of mind

Happiness for all eternity

Love

I love you more than life itself

This poem is a symbol of my heart

Not just a card that sits on a shelf

You, me, baby

Us as three

Our family is the most important thing

You are the glue that holds us together

Daughter as your princess

Wife as your queen

My man the husband

As our king

I wear my heart on my sleeve

Remember I will always love you

Just believe…

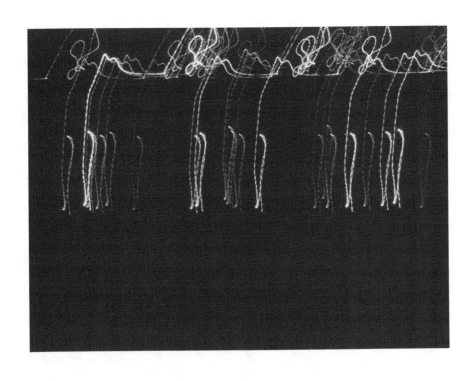

Magic

When magic flows through a simple cosmic touch

The feeling of tingles came upon my heart

It's not just a day dream it means so much

I can open myself up to a new start

Treasure those magical moments and such

Allow the happiness in, never depart

Magic isn't just an illusion, you'll see

Magic is real and it means so much to me

It's not imaginary it's what you believe

And what you believe is the truth inside

The truth inside is something hard to conceive

Conceiving magic upon the world it lied

Love is magic, that's what I want to achieve

Wonderful tears of happiness I cried

Hoping you love me as much as I love you

At first there was one and now there is two

Mineral Springs

Maybe this is the start of something great
Internalizing your own self worth
No interruptions, secluded
Euphoria and enchantment, makes its way
Reality pushed through, listen to what your heart is telling you
Alone but together
Love is in the making

Scared but excited
Person, to person, learning about each other
Remember to have faith
Insight towards the future
Numerous glances across the room
Great man may care about me
Savor the feeling for all time and eternity

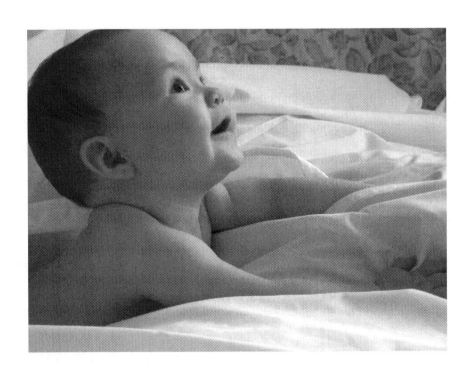

My Baby Girl

Baby oh baby by

Unconditional love will come from daddy and I

An idea she once was, a reality she is

An overwhelming feeling of emotions and bliss

I have been wishing upon a star for you to come to me

Be born happy and healthy, I can't wait to see

Holding you in my arms for the first time

I shall cry

Baby oh bay by

My Fairytale

A man and a woman both gazing into each other's eyes
My heart starts beating rapidly
My body chemistry magnifies
A sensation starts to the tips of my toes
To the ends of my hair
I shall imbed this wonderful feeling into my heart
And shelter it with care
That's love…
I'm in love with you
I found my man
I found my prince
My knight in shining armor
I shall love you forever
Love me through my imperfections of being human
Cherish the person I am…
Me
Forever and all eternity
I will love you always
Through the darkest of days
And the sleepless nights
As I awake in the morning
Arms wrapped around me bound so tight
You fulfilled my fairytale
Share your heart with me
Let your dreams become mine
Now I know you are not just a dream
Because you touched my soul and made it shine

Nephew's of Mine

All of them will grow up to be handsome and strong
With their knowledge they will grow up to learn right from wrong
They will experience everlasting love
With their free spirit, they will sour through a
Beautiful untouched sky like an independent
And disguised dove
Men shall they grow up to be
Will honor and dignity
You will...
Feel
Taste
Achieve
Dream
Discover   ...things
Play
Create
Imagine
&
Explore
Withhold these qualities in your heart
And never ignore
They will be leaders of their own free world
They will Have many special gifts
With the ribbon curled
Gavin work hard in life
Love and achieve
Cameron live life to the fullest
See things and believe
Evan remember your keen heart
Feel joy and happiness in your soul to conceive
Dylan with each new day stand tall and proud
The sun shall rise upon every eve

One Spring Day

Sun shining on a bright warm day

Could be March,

Could be June,

I think it's the month of May

As I'm driving in my car, windy sky

Blowing spring peddles through the air

All you see looking left,

Looking right,

Energy of smiles as I glance and stare

Walking along the sidewalk,

Watching and viewing

Smelling the ocean water and the sparkling reflection

Is refreshing and renewing

Spring seasons align

Plants grow from the sunshine

This days happiness is all mine

Peace

Peace is sense of tranquility

To be silent, but be heard

Being secluded allows our subconscious to rest

Thinking about what is right

And what is real

Later as we answer our own questions

Is when our soul is at best

Pure Bliss

Bliss is a feeling of spiritual joy

Small moments in time that should be captured with no hesitation

Soaking in warm water with illuminating light from a candle

Thinking of who and what you love

Trophies and pictures sitting on the mantel

Warm sunny day in August

Flip flops and a tank top

Walking along the boardwalk, cool breezy air from the corner shop

Enjoying friendships and contagious smiles

Children laughing while sitting behind 25 cent lemonade stand

Sharing sweet summer juice with neighbors for miles and miles

While riding a horse you have strength and independence

You are on top of the world

Open fields and pastures balancing you with confidence

Seasons

Spring
Warm showers
Colorful flowers blooming
Peaceful, lovely, and hopeful
April, May

Summer
Hot sun
Rippling water sailing
Energetic, happiness, and excitement
June, July

Fall
Autumn leaves
Crisp afternoon walk
Grateful, tranquil, and intriguing
September, October

Winter
Snow falling
Sitting by the fire
Joy, spiritual, and delighted
November, December

Snowmobiling

A magnificent snowmobile
Left turns must kneel,
View the snow bed
In a blue sled.

Adrenalin hits in the heart
Going like a dart,
Driving in trails
Sharp turn then bails.

Snow falling in your face,
Put visor in place.
Keeping up too,
Enjoy the view.

Surfing

Riding waves is all about a state of mind
Balancing on the board and staying aligned
Listening in the tube, thoughts gathering in your den
Found your place of peace and Zen

The ocean has empathy for one's self
It's a place you lose yourself and find yourself
Obsession for that natural high is pure adrenaline
Found your place of peace and Zen

A swell of elegance, that continuous wave
Riding nature's beast is so brave
You will always want to surf again and again
Found your place of peace and Zen

Thinking

Trying to be **aware** of what my heart is telling me
Having **concern** of what the future has in store
I live in an ocean of **consciousness**
Nurturing what you **care** most about
Knowing whom you are **inside** is the most important
I've felt the **apprehension** of the unknown
Now knowing the **realization** that everything happens for a reason
Grasping the **recognition** that you are special

Thinking in the Coffee Shop

Sitting down drinking my coffee not needing anymore

Thinking about what my future has in store

Remembering that old boyfriend that would always ignore

Missing surfing along Westport's shore

Wanting a new job, not like the one before

Waiting for the waitress, I need another pour

Reading this book I'm about to the core

Glancing at this handsome man, wondering if there could be more

New thought in mind, should I keep sitting here or talk to him, I'm tore

Looked at my watch it's time to go, wow he opened the door

Time to be Free

It's time to be free

Your heart has been hurt and now is closed

Now sacrificing your soul once again

The personality of someone to need you was once opposed

It's time to be free

Take chances yet have faith

Find yourself within this world

You will experience hard times but God will keep you safe

It's time to be free

Believe in the people you care about

Try and trust the things you don't

Having the attitude of willfulness being stout

Your will to live is what sets you free

So just be

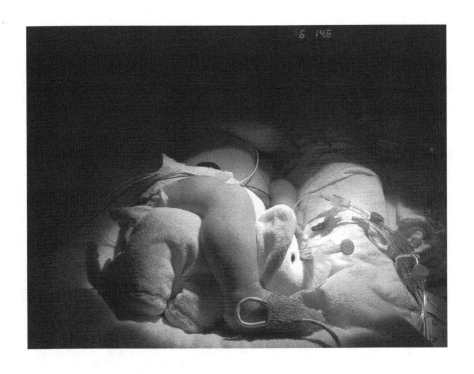

Toy Rattle

Her first cry

Laying on my belly

Having to say goodbye

Her first strenuous instinct to breathe

Tears flew swift

Wiping away from my sleeve

Her first helicopter ride

In the incubator she lied

As she lies on her side, to breathe is a battle

For comfort she has her soft toy rattle

Another week goes by

Her health was significantly low

And now is considerably high

A healthy baby homeward bound

Peace was once lost and now is found

Unique

Why try so hard to fit in

When you were born to stand out

Being happy and unique

Is what it should be all about

The human race evolved

With perfect images to be

Living in a cynical world

Still held with your heart,

Honor and dignity

The beauty of your soul is quite rare

Granted your personality inside

You should share

You stand out

This is what uniqueness,

Is all about

Water Woman

The deepest inner reflection of your senses

Envision a new life looking through those lenses

Relax, breathe easy, float and fall

Wrap your emotions in that black shall

Imagine you are in your favorite place

Portray a soft face

Who is She

She is a woman
A woman named Melissa
Beautiful, elegant, smart
She opened her soul to the world
The world gave her hard self-image inside
Trying to put the pieces together
How?...
With a broken heart
As she grew older
She became stronger
Inspirational, loving and real
Her eyes look upon you as a gift
With a seal
Some worlds are stressful and sad
Some worlds are wonderful
And make you deliriously glad
One day the clouds were upon her
Rained her tears
The winds poured from her soul
The warm sun prevailed
Spoke to her and gave
All she needs is her family
To fill her heart

Wondering Wilderness

Fragile fences, furry fellow…

Mossy mound, mountain mellow…

Marvelous miles, mystic moat…

Fantastic frontier, forest float…

Somber smog, shallow sight…

Weeping willow, weather white…

Whispering water, wilderness ways…

Serene shadows, spring stays…

Refreshing rain, river right…

Legendary lakeshore, luminous light…

Listening land, leaf lays…

Radiant region, refined rays…

World

Dark gray skies

Soft sandy beaches

Hot black concrete on your feet in deep June

Bright warm sunshine

Cold ocean water

The reflection in your eyes

Looking at the glowing moon

The world as it is

The world at its best

The world where you live your life

Life is happiness

Life is responsibility

Life is devotion

Life is honesty

Life is exciting

Life is hard

But…

Life is amazing

You are amazing, you are my life

And a part of my world

World Breathes

The world breathes through its beauty

It cries through the rain

It smiled when your existence became

As the moon shines through the dark blue blanket in the sky

It reminds me of that compassionate twinkle in your eye

You shall be free

You will fly high at the edge of the sky

God gave me to you

The world gave you to me

Kindness, love, charity, understanding

And above all friendship

You are my world, my best friend

My mother and love you forever